The Master Thief

Camille Guthrie

Camille Guthrie
2·10·02

THE MASTER THIEF

A poem in twelve parts

Subpress

2000

This book is for Duncan

Acknowledgements

Grateful acknowledgement is made to the editors of the following publications, in which poems in this book first appeared, many in earlier drafts: *The Impercipient, Black Bread, Talisman, Explosive, 6ix, 13th Moon,* and *The Transcendental Friend.*
"It Was a Ghost" and "Riddling Tales" were published as a section of *re: Chapbook 3* (reference: press, 1997).
"The Old Woman of the Forest" and "The Servant" first appeared in *An Avec Sampler 1998.*

The author wishes to express her gratitude to Karen, Robert, Meghan, and Rob Guthrie for love and home; to Erika Mijlin for fearless friendship; to C.D. Wright and Keith Waldrop for enthusiasm; to Mike Scharf for comradeship; to Justine Kurland for generosity; and to Beth Anderson for shared adventure.

Cover photography by Justine Kurland. Cover design by Erika Mijlin.

Subpress
2955 Dole Street
Honolulu, Hawai'i 96816

Subpress books are available from Small Press Distribution, Inc.:
(800) 869-7553
orders@spdbooks.org

Contents

The Marked Child

The Marked Child begins a dangerous voyage— The argument of Fast & Loose— She's Big With performs twelve labors— Riddling Tales— The Old Woman of the Forest— The Animal tells a ceaseless tale— It was a Ghost— The Girl in the Machine— The Girl Without Hands meets her demon— The Servant's Reply— Night— Some account of that journey, and the difficulties the Author was in— And then, the Master Thief ends

Already here, in a beginning
There lies room in a garden for rupture
And names in a basin of attraction
Spiral on the finer scales

Chains of events, green chains of everything
Now admit the immigrant in
Drawing water, with a portmanteau
Secreting corporeal surrogates

Rowing towards the horizon
Towards distant jagged shores
Whose story ingeminates
And familiar dress grows porous

I'm my primeval size — half-full
Spinning indeterminate hazes
Small drafts and their erratic expanse
I'm exaggerating a little

If a mind finds ancestral sustenance
Astonishing its imperfect inertia
Surely to translate tenders ambivalence
Laboring a liquid measuring cup

We detected something in the distortion
Plates stacked and spilled dynamic
An era shelved in portions
The entropy of its apple — scares me

Child land escapes frantic
Charted away to ritual pastures
I didn't — didn't remain an impostor
In the vagrant playground

Now give me more
Than this experiment wrecked
This bullet expressed
This apron stained and untied

Memory as a wish is restless
Choosing excess, sorting necessity
I'm a listener and will not whisper
That is not my name

Muchness is noted
Muchness is barefoot
Have I the density?
Do I the degrees?

What amasses—a collapse
Atom upon bone upon
Fluid upon once
Upon the dark matter among us

And it's rare balm I'm calling upon
A girl wanders, girl without means
If only it fit. Oh do let me undo it
In a conversation that's a real forest

Fast & Loose

So she said yes and put her hand in his hand — *Snippety-snap* — Fast & Loose vital currents began to circulate — The particulars of the inheritance — A number of wild useful plants — "How dare you sneak into my garden like a thief! I'll make you pay dearly for this" — Oh, that I had a letter! — A further account of the mistake — Which way? Which way?

Girl is a name upon a time
This can go on as long as you like
I knew all the words by heart
And they were all very happy

Now go on as you like:
They went into the house
They were very, very happy
They sat down at the table

Like it? Once into the house
As usual, they all ate
Pulling chairs up to the table
Singing, "It is the beginning"

What was it they all ate?
The beginning, always the hardest
To swallow. In the beginning
I'll never be able to do that

Since to begin is hardest
When sewn into a nightgown
(She'll never be able to get out of that)
Or into a pair of slippers

What? A person sewn into a gown?
Yes. It's a kind of formal combat
With what? With slippers?
Yes. The right was marked with her father's name

(Which is his kind of formal combat)
And on the left was written her own name

(Not quite the same as his name —
Now look!) Beside the bed, a letter

On which was written her name
It was a new idea to her
Sitting beside the bed, opening the letter:
"You know very well you're not real."

What a new idea to her-
Who-insisted, "I don't get the message:
'You very well know you're not real.'
And I don't like belonging to another's dream"

Insistent, trying to get the message
Looking quietly down at her foot
Thinking, "I hate other people's dreams"
As blood began spurting from her shoe —

She stared, startled, at her bright foot
There, staining her white stocking red
Blood spilled from her small shoe
(Let's just wait, see what happens)

Stained there, on her stocking, she read:
"This is my story, I've reread it"
Now you can see what has happened
As the mouth who last told this is still warm

This then is my story, just try to read it
And know the words by heart
The mouth who tells you this is warm
Girl is my name, once and at times

The Argument

I loved him, I loved
And was not ashamed
However, somebody was implicated
That's clear, at any rate

The rare flower pluck'd
A mantle in twain

Then, somebody who'd found an old key
Did not require a new one

Roocoo Roocoo
There's blood in my shoe

Father, I should like
Eleven companions exactly like myself
In face, figure, and size

Then the girls put them on
And I myself donned the last suit

Now you are mine and I am yours
No one in the world can change that

(And there's a whole language
Concealed in this thought)

So the servant, well disposed
To the hunters went to them
And disclosed the project:

One killed none, yet killed twelve
What is it?

They looked into their books
But it wasn't there, in short
The riddle was too much for them

Besides, she's she and I'm I
O dear, o monstrous act
It is the cause, the

Moment of desire! The motion
Of desire, my soul, hear her

Woes and echo back her cries

Roocoo

So on we went

O

dimmed path and minor root

Poor scout now sound out

this barefoot adventure

Tally-ho! and over and back

You and I shall always talk together so

Chains of evidence

and green chains of everything

The Twelve Labors

Promised with Vision— She's Big With performs twelve labors—
Goes forth to learn what Fear was— Making the Beds— Sifting the
Sea— A Monstrous Act— The Fallen Leaves— Sharing Joy and
Sorrow— The Twelve White Shirts— A Kind of Torture— A
Bargain— Thee-then-no-me— The Two Exits— But is it Useful?—
By-the-by she fails and leaves barefoot

I went forth to learn what Fear was
What it eats, who it knows, how it does
Ah, if I could but shudder
How closer I'd come to father & mother

Turn back, young maiden dear
'Tis a murderer's house you enter here
Dost understand the word?

Well, knitting through sky & water this bird
Inscribes its stunning radius
With throes of Arctic indifference
Gripping a random key in the sun
Fear's a calamity of translation
Since none puts by   *Browning*
The zero I have drawn for you, but I—
I feel it drill a fever into me
Another thermometer of Humility

Very Good

24

Bed-Maker, the bed's again undone
From blank to blank, tuck and straighten

The accident, my everlasting duty
To arrange another's privacy
And perfect comfort—but so futile
Is this blanketed ritual:
Always shoes beneath a remoter bed,
And mattress upon soiled mattress piled
Over me, reluctantly witnessing
Another weight, rudely stirring
Yet another contract sealed, or barely
Perceived—Seamless ecstasy—
Mighty contests rise from trivial things
In good nights and good mornings—
If not for this one persistent irritant
Then that illegitimate occupant
Cock-a-doodle-doo
Your dirty girl's come back to you

No

Now sift the sea of its impurities

A vast impossibility —
So I married, deflowered on a river bed
By an eager shark — Together, our flood
Whelmed volumes, poured shores — We distilled
Ten maelstroms through one hundred glass funnels —
But a history of drift and spillage
Prevented clearing even one blotted passage
O poison's boiling shipwreck
Your fluent faucet only reflects
Longitudes & latitudes of death
Then the Great Catch-Basin said:
"Who drinks of me shall be a liar
Who drinks of me shall be a failure"
Frightened, I hid in the mazey depth
Holding my bride's breath
But my husband rolled, poor beast
Defeated, tearing himself to pieces
Thus, I relinquished my cup of sun

And on and on

Just this or that in you
Disgusts me — whether you resist, or swallow
Here you miss, or there exceed the mark

Eliot

No thing disturbs me from this work
Or could lift my curious forehead —
Tho' ample receptacle, a girl unfed
Feeds a wound's convulsive pleasure
Fluttring her throat over a floor —
Upset's shining bowl, devoured whole
Portions food for malreversal
Interrupted by a table's trembling grimace —
My figure's arrested, all diminished
By forks & knives, my life is punctuated
By a spoon dropped, a mouth hesitated
O monstrous act!
I throw up a line and seize it right back

Now

Go into the woods and confront the tree
Whose fallen leaves made us guilty

I found it, thousands of years old
So thick, four elephants could not hold
Its beastly trunk, and so many birds built nests
In its branches, many-colored birds, so many voices
I dropped my ax—O let them be left
All this wild wilderness and wet!
Only myself will fall, and into sand ambitions sink
(My guilt was surely an acquired instinct)
I came here for a cure, here to prove
Right that loosener, Love—
Suddenly appeared a friend I relied on often
(Certain instincts we had in common:
Emotion—Language—Reason—Imagination—Curiosity—
Abstraction—Self-consciousness—Memory—Sense of Beauty)
Without warning, Nakedness
Rose out of Chaos
In our sudden Sexual Selection
The laws of unity and the condition
Of existence was embraced
My face facing his face...
But he ran, unknowing this powerful root
Lives underground, and new branches there

Shoot

Remember the stepmother
Branded a thief like the others
Who died an evil death? Traitor's
Blood streams by acres —
Now into her blood dip your arrow
In order to share joy and sorrow

This labor suggests the ultimate
Sympathy: my own private bullet
See-sawing upon a river of stains
Bailing the overflowing remains —
So my barefoot rank is Empathy
Resisting an arc of tyranny
And the advance of alarm
Flaying victim upon victim —
Will we remain, will we perish
In this hint of apocalypse?
But I cannot bear Atlas's burden —
Won't you lend me a cushion?

The girl will not do it

Forfeit

Use industry, use scrutiny
Keep the shirts as white as white can be

I willingly tend to no other
If by doing so I can serve my twelve brothers,
Smoothing wrinkles with a flashing iron
Hands bleached as an apparition
I'll bend for my inheritance
Preserving their pressing business...
But one day, feeling fanciful & silly
I plucked all the bright garden lilies
While my brothers' shirts dried, empty as sails —
Yet the twelfth emerged frozen from the well
I just couldn't melt its rigid collar —
It blinked in the sun, sterile and formal
Thus, the brothers were changed into
Twelve ravens, and hitherto
The house and garden likewise vanished
Leaving only their long promise:
"We swear to avenge ourselves by the morrow
Wherever we find a girl, red blood shall flow"

Do not proceed

Now you must be dumb for seven years
And may not speak, laugh or show fear
If you utter a single word, all is in vain
And your only childhood fame
Will be this one reward:
Your brothers will be killed by the one word

I said in my heart, I know with certainty
I shall set my brothers free
By constructing a small prosthesis
To confine my senses into a form of crisis —
Fashion each syllable, muzzle every figure
Into a mask of timidity and stupor —
So I played dumb
Waiting, watching the steel pendulum
Pierce twelve twice a day — paralyzed
By any guess of distress or noise
Be cautious,
Mine Anonymous
Only your incessant modesty
Blesses your brothers' liberty

Clamped in this jar, in this jar strapped
She never laughed

Continue

Come live with me and be my love
And we will all the pleasures prove   Herrick

No, dear Huntsman, do let me live
Alone, but two little ones I'll give
A girl and boy, my body will express
For your fill of youth and loveliness —
As he accepted this compromise
My bargain I set out to justify,
Nearby fear and distant from bliss
I found a volunteer, eager and nameless
All the while, regretful of that I swore
Full of pity, hard pity for my visitors
Who myself they will speak and spell
In nine months, in every way tell
Of their origin, house and unhouse
The secret, for I would not a spouse
Be — Yet they were not willing to go
At birth, they would not be parted — so
I wished they be changed
Into two roses, and in exchange
For the bargain, the afterbirth I left
Blood brilliant, and fleeing swift

But you promised

So the author and the huntsman felt cheated

Although I groveling pleaded
They infected the children's blankets
And this tradition killed — in an instant —
Paused, I scratched their names with a ring
On their bedroom window, with wing
Of bright grief, covered my face
With the red dress of rage
Aged in an hour, aged a thousand years
Years? I mean lives, heavy hours
Buckle and break happy, happy love!
The mastery of the thing, the achieve of
Leaving my brief guests at the scene —
Rest quietly in the quiet, leafy ravine
Where I will not go — Cry I can no more
I can *something*, can find what's the matter
Even if veiled, even if I'm a failure

A failure

One Afflicts, One's Exquisite

A sign said at the cave with two exits
I chose the only exit one could
(Blurry and disarming as a childhood)
Knowing I'd be punished for years
By being drowned in my own tears—
Suppose we change the subject
I'm getting so very tired, I object—
Ed—I vote the author tell *me* a story
Nonsense! the author then flurried:
You know you have your little crimes:
You make your own face, and not your own rhymes—
Admit, do you say what you mean?
Or do you only recite what you've already seen?
And, of what is your little life made?
I'm not sure... Nothing but empty shade?
(Instead of applause, she sent in the bill)
Now I wished I hadn't cried so much, I'll
Never be able to pay for all of this,
So I waded through the watery evidence—

You swim about, trying to find your way

Out

I took the Promise in my hand
Into dense thickets I ran –
Said aloud, "I must report
The truth, bring back some part
Of the fruits of my labors, bring it back alive"
But all my failures I cannot leave
Outside formality's gates,
Outside What-cannot-be, I cried to my fate,
"Have you brought what you have promised me?
Who has ever completed such deeds?
And tell me now, of what use am I?"

Not for immortality's wisdom –
    For barefoot vision.

Riddling Tales

When she returned, her key no longer fit in the door— Alone now, traveling, she meets a Wrecker— Free-tongued, it reaches for her hand— "Sound me out with precise words— I will not speak my mystery if you hide that of which you have deepest knowledge— Did not Heraclitus say: One cannot be bitten by the same author twice?"— They exchange riddling tales— The difference in mental powers immense— More answers

MORE ANSWERS

Bell, Swan, Barnacle goose, Submarine earthquake, Ten chickens, Urges to draw, Mouth or Bridge?, Cuttlefish? Siren?, Bagpipe, Iceberg, Ship (with perplexing code lang.), Bellows, A long conversation, The Butterfly Alphabet, Created things (incomplete), Pen and three fingers, The New Suit, The Androgyne, The first sign one is on the right path, The Haunted Hotel, The Pencil Driver, Bookcase or Oven?, Crows? Swallows? Loons?, Much Madness? (untranslatable), A Beaker, A Moth, Artist's ambition, Enemies of truth, Bright curiosity, The Twelve Gates, Fish and river, The key to immortality?, (Uncertain, imperfect), A wandering singer?

The Old Woman of the Forest

An abandoned house— How can it have gotten there?— The next thing is to get into that garden— There lives the Old Woman of the forest— She lures wild beasts and birds to her— And kills and boils and roasts them— Convergence of character— An apology— Skills in Musick— Drawing in the dust

The house was there, the house was abandoned

Where are you?
Wading through the dust of the hallway
Here in the kitchen, a voice said, *I'm boiling the water*

Nobody was in the kitchen, only a rusted pot

From the bottom of the collapsed stairs
Where are you?

I'm here in the bathroom, brushing my hair
But no one was there and the mirror glared

Where are you really?
Here I am in bed taking a nap

Sure enough someone had been sleeping
But she was too late, the sheets were tossed

Here I am in the garden
I have a message for you

Through a bleary window
bending over a riot of weeds,
It was an old woman

But first,
Open the window and let the lies out

Roocoo Roocoo
There's blood in my shoe
The foot's too long
The foot's too wide
That's not the proper bride

Roocoo Ri Coo
There's dust in my shoe
The trial's too long
The trial's too wide
That's not the original bride

Roocoo Coo
There's ink in my shoe
The book's too long
The book's too wide
That's not the possible bride

The girl understood but began to cry

You are upset, let me sing you another song

Is it very long?

It's long, but very significant

Here lies Nobody
Stirring & flung
In time in time

A child's paper mask
I bear, I read
The message boldly:
"We are relations"

A stranger truth
Seized — though simple
A wrestled vision

Here mistakes translate
"She was false as water"

All cry shame against me
Carrying an ancient suitcase
So I took it, chose it

I'm really very sorry
But I was rudely forced
By necessity by
That boy Immortality

Ah, all the married forces
All the little lines
Now flee!
To the faceted sea

You must now take courage
And listen without fail
And judge tenderly of me

The horror of this moment
I will never forget

You will though
If you don't make a note of it

So she began to draw in the dirt

I can't manage my hand at all
It writes all sorts of things I don't intend:

"One killed none
Yet killed twelve, find me"

You just have to get used to it
It's the beginning
And that's always the hardest

The Animal

The Animal tells a minor tale— The beginning of another end— Her being kidnapped— Marking his initials— She flees and is changed— The stream swells with tears— Enter the monster's spectacular eyes— A single darkness— So-ho! Original shape is restored— A name in the dust— Alas, Immortality

A Fiction
its carousing course

Shifting one heavy foot
to the other setting

Falls through Caesura's sieve
and avalanches of minutes

My tale told

punctually rending
already torn rhythms

The years the
great abstract tomorrow

Character captured
at the hinge of two destinies

While still unhandseled
When water was precise

Fissure articulate

Limniad eclipsed

You are fit for the shady grove

Vernal, or irresistible
I stepped into his radius

In the blink of its chance
In the bed of his maelstrom

Carved twelve times
his initials into my stipling side

Alas, cried my father
Even as a cow she was lovely

Leaves of trees

were my food
and bitter grasses

I drank from
muddied waters

Instead of
a bed I lay
on ground

not always grassy

I fled from myself
So-ho and back again

His whole hundred
Impeccable eyes on guard

Littoral
my plotted vigil

Suddenly the light
of his many eyes was quenched

In a single darkness he lay dead
Starry-eyed I traced letters

In the dust
Distant pastures

Raise the here and cry
Returned to my true form

Afraid to speak in case
I should low like a heifer

While the fury remains, chasing me
chasing me towards Immortality

Eventually I could not remember

the Menace I disguised
all my fears into masked figures

The subject's vapors were lost
helically drawn

Towards simpler equations

One occasionally
hammers at my marbled ankles
and I drag the antiquary
through volumes, voids

Your innocencies
busy in the molting present
cannot grasp the scaling

of danger
or crude readings:

If I submit to
the author of authors

Before you can say,
The Be-All

I'm at the bright mouth
of the tyger

Catching fire

Blake

Memoried,

my irrelevant
alluvium

I speak from

the promiscuous quietus

never identical
ever in green shade

It Was a Ghost

From this hand-me-down, some evidence— [*Enter the ghost.*]—
Surprise at seeing a little bone— Out of it, she carved a mouth-
piece— The bone began of itself to sing: Now I will show myself to
you in my true form— Witness to a thorough wet day— Her wonder
at what books she was to carry— Pages gather by ingenious means
and are distilled— Wanting to be familiar with her extremity— Yet
there, the Matter ends

Draw, write, read
Read King Lear, draw
Dear lake! I shall ever love thee
Mary reads, and eats oranges

Shakespeare

Put the room to rights
A letter from my father, a fine thunder shower
Disgusting dreams have occupied the night

Write my story and translate
I repeated one of my own poems
Those that love cannot separate

S. sees my name in Milton
A very grim dream, unwell, take medicine, lie down
Bonaparte invades France
This is a day devoted to Love in idleness

Transcribe, after dinner, walk in the garden
Write Preface. Finis.
We talk, study a little Greek, and go to bed
This is repeated throughout the week

When baffling winds struck the sails
[*Here are several leaves torn out.*]
Find my baby dead. A miserable day

When baffling winds struck the sails
I was a mother, and am so no longer
None care to read my sorrow
[*Here a good deal torn out.*]

Get up, Shelley, the sea is flooding the house
And it is all coming down

And on its passing she was no longer visible
The watery surface was a blank

Do you know anything of Shelley?
But I am chained to time and cannot thence depart

This solitude of endless pines

Why cannot you answer me, my own one?
Is the instrument so utterly damaged?
I am reduced to these white pages
I am to blot with dark imagery

Grief at least tells me I was not always what I am now
As it is, I am torn to pieces by memory

Little, truly have I to fear
Books do much, but the living intercourse is the vital heat
Activity of spirit is my sphere

My imagination, my Kubla Khan, my pleasure dome   *Coleridge*
Occasionally pushed aside by misery
But at first opportunity her beaming face peeped in

I said I lead an innocent life
It may become a useful one

What can I do? How change my destiny?
By what be conquered? To whom cede?
My mind gathers wrinkles
What will become of me?

Thus, I have put down my thoughts
I may have deceived myself

I go to no new Creation
I enter under no new laws

The Girl in the Machine

Excursion into the Interior— Rudimentary structures, muscles, sense-organs, hair, bones, reproductive organs, &c— The use or disuse of parts— Tools and weapons used by the Animals— Organs of extreme perfection— Organs of little importance— And Organs not in all cases absolutely perfect— The importance of this corporeal structure— How things she formed of a formelesse mass

Knit-knit-knit
my silvery business
see part cut apart
blood edits no limit
in my moving chair

Patch eye latch
and gloss the sockets
pin lens then stitch
the flickering stock

or this extra amiss
or this electric kiss

O bandaged animal
INTERRUPTING
mechanical hurt
perpetual skirt

The whole some
body be traveled

So bolt it and
wrench what renders

bitter mal-reversal
I cried the entire way
for the true conjugate

I flee
over a dreadful fury
over purity-depravity

All the overheard lines
and airs in the trees

My staircase goes on
I have no fear I go

But this door opens one-way
Pity me pity
knit-knit

The Girl Without Hands

Now accused of thievery— The Girl without Hands leaves— More trades— Acquired instincts— The help of a servant— Difficulties with the demon— An heir, an invention— Effects of climate— Unfortunate quotations— Some hints concerning the origin of the demon, with the opinions of different authors— A delicious meal— Many partings

Accused of any little thing, wronged by my peers, I confessed
shedding beautiful tears on my hands.

My sentence read, the hatchet flashed,
my two hands buried at the root.

I knew I could not stay. I cast far—for weeks on end
inhabiting the pines, looking in lakes
until collapsing finally on a peculiar lawn.

A face. Scenery. A man's leafy promises:
"If you can love me by the morrow,
I will make you a new pair of hands."

What was I to do?
                                    I said, "I will,"
and pulled dresses from acorn shells.

The servant called for my demon,
and we waited patiently in the Pears-have-all-been-Counted garden—

It materialized,
carefully cutting out my spitting heart.

                    I fainted. A ghost

of a protest, and left
a watermark on the entranceway.

The first year pared round its sorry burdens
at my expense. I waved new glass hands.
Summer was similar: slow action, battery of beaded days.
Knuckling under my lines, I was scalded by the glare.

So the enchanter suggested another trade: my spine for a newborn child.

A hard bargain,
but I shook hands and Emilia, the servant,
yanked the reluctant scorpion from its lair.

Gobbling now lust in action
the demon yelled, *Engraft yourself*
and ran for the humming hills.

Betweenpie, I expected the loveliest brainchild ever.

I grew fond of those months, the streaming particles
flagging air and water, myself, elemental.
I was left numbed by the unknown origin of domestic productions.

Then, in the mother of months —
in an instant, an infant
discharged in a shower of wet.
It was a lonelier thing than any I've seen.

By self-example, his were blue glass eyes
so sullen and utterly mirrory,
baby's sadness killed us outright with looks.

Baby and I, upright
navigated our vast lawn
in a steely image of my initial self,
a wheeling silver chair, a ticking metronome.

And when Spring threw a lime-spray foam from the trees
(misted with sighs, salted with mist) my foundling
feigned a miracle.

       He walks.
                Sways —

Yet how I longed for my word-for-word memory
so glazed, broken, not withstanding
the eyelet hopes.
I winced
suggesting disaster,

"My tongue, for a chance to name you?"
Call me by my name, I'll come to it.

Still the season still dazzled
with icy intractables.
I lacked, I caught
colds, kept them in china cups.
From crippling glitter
I collected grudges: Winter's indifferent.

And every night, the same dream

Chalked cliff embedding
my body into unexcavated bones
all my nostalgias pitch
past pitched waves

Shoving me over

and you,

arrive, hair wet & your long hands

What happened laps

at the shore of

the difference that exists

between us, and then

the sea effaces it.

Soon, soon
the Fall shot its red metals
through my shoulder-blades
then flayed all the leaves.

I toed the grain.
Awake now, and nobody home
except lures piled behind doorways,
meaning digested the while
and spit up a glint which fell
into the guileless grasses.

Look — there — Was it much too late?
No. We had to do what we had to do.

In pursuit, naming names

"Aminadab, Archimago, Automedusa?"

No. That is not my name.

"Moloch, Mulciber, Mephisto, Muttonchop?"

No, that isn't my name.

"Sansjoy? Ratman? Creature of the Deep? Ouroboros?"

Simpler than that.

"Troubled Youth? Lil' Vagabond?
Inkspiller, Tattle-tale, Poorfist?"

"Those Slipping Scalpels? Twelfth Night?"

"Nobodaddy? Boy-Zeus? Behemoth Rex?"

No —

"The Beast that was, is not, and yet is?"

Now give me what you promised.

I had had all I could stand.

I must kill the little me which kills

me, murder by degrees

hurtling my chair
pinning it down,
cutting it to pieces.

Swift Emilia, scissors & thread
repaired my former self. O familiar
bright wet heart
knocking back in cavern. I gushed —

she said, "Keep still," and slid the spine in.

How like a human, I stand, and walk about

I felt my life with both my hands.

Then, with a stitch, my tongue.

The whole of it

The whole of it

came not at once, but in bowls
fragrant, steaming, it was ready.

We drank to the very bottom of my remains.

I swallowed my own striking tail.

Little we knew
this was my child's last meal. He cried
through faceted-glass tears,
"'Tis life's award!"

And my husband? Emilia too
abandoned ship. I knew not

but my own hands, so I packed my belongings
and drove far from what

some have called experience.

The Servant's Reply

10

The servant of the master— Or the master of the servant— Natural selection— Its power on characters of small importance— The causes which led to her becoming Islands volcanic— Various instances of deception, cruelty and lies— Her heart upon a little plate— Ekphrasis, the Author's distress— Is wounded by the arrows— She would not let that copy die

Emilia at the door.

EMILIA

What did your song bode?

THE GIRL WITHOUT HANDS [*Sings within*]

Go to
Warm need hem ruin
Mop slaps blot pride and organize smells

Mow tension sweep threats paste question
Scissor fear iron tears and make

Sweet, sweet make

Then rake mistake poach plan whisk guest
Wipe lies drain envy weed nerves

Vacuum worry endeavor shadow
Obey Baby and

Charm your tongue

EMILIA

Right away.

EMILIA [*aside*]

Give the lie
My female evil

Playing parent's part, you
Only kiss kindness. Come on,
Admit impediments, show the choice

Myself I forfeit
To be parent's sweet counterfeit.
Above my bedroom door
In red letter, read:
FREE TODAY, TOMORROW PAY

So pay the whole
Now root pity
On that false borrowed face:
Villainy! I hate
From hate away you throw

Save my life saying, "Not you
Anymore," not you, anymore

Though bound to you
By barren rhyme and bound
To you by the barest matter

My-next-self
Travels Distant Pastures
Travels   Aflame

Night

11

Night— Flung towards the great attractor— Three remarkable
dreams— The woods where things have no name— Profound
ravines— A storm described— Narrowly escapes drowning in a suc-
cession of waterfalls— There plant *One-eye, Two-eyes, Three-eyes*—
Manners of its Phaenomenon— Enchanted, the words flew about the
room— All else changes on invisibly finer scales

From whence do you come
& whither are you bound

from whence do you come
& whither are you bound

Allied to all degrees of shadow

Your storm of colors takes off on spiral wings

Vast lace-like disturbances
Tempests tossed from a seahorse tail

Now count them all
On inexorably strange scaling structures

Ah the way is too long & what shall I do

In a dynamical land where I am unknown

I lay down on a bed of glass

Small hand mirrors examined my lunar profile

When the giant imprinted its spine into my palm

The size of a black heron

Youhavealwayshadsuchbeautifuleyes

Pop-pop

goes the owl's own code

Pop

went the butterfly mask

Nosoonerhadthecombtouchedherhair

She fell asleep and so foliaged

Furred hour bed of branch abreast of

Thoughtsense   Thoughtdust

loamyhumming

drowninglily

Climbs the stairs

through webs of eyelids, pulled ideas of webs

You must proceed   *wave*   *ily*

Ocean's prism

Emotion's infusoria

What did the Occhiale see?
Stellectric chains of mercurial events
Yet it observed flawlessly

Waves leapt to the margin of the basin also from the midnight mare's racing spine I crept into steep feeling and into the arms of gravity my lost force come it said let me lace you up properly come it said laces all colors and sizes

Loaded onto a blue skiff

my reflection doubling

floats by impenetrable canopies
floats by all my maidenheads

Culled from the debris Timewards, to a
sub-umb
ilical pre-
cipice

            Pop

                              Pop

The typewriter turned to me and spoke,
It was only a paper pistol.

Adding, *She didn't rot*
but continued to look as if asleep.

CANDLE OR PENCIL

RESEMBLANCE IS

NO MERE ACCIDENT

IN A SPARKLING WIND

WORDS FLEW

ABOUT THE ROOM

A pile of wandered-through sleeves
Of safety pins torn from hems

A pile of articulate bullets
Of lashes immersed in salt

Of silver blades as though dead
Of braids knit from pure reason

One-Eye Two-Eyes Three-Eyes
Of suitcases flapping wings

Adrowse

ORDER

                    swiftly emerges

Intricate typestry of names
Diffuse sheets of spheres slung wide
Rose out of chaos

Yet forgetting the original equation

Have I changed in the night?

Little   by   little

she   came   to

The Master Thief

Finally, and at last The Master Thief ends—

If lost in the failing forest light
Drifting in a barren dream
She was found—she wore
Her rue with a difference

A real nobody
She bore a pleated rage
Disobedient seam
Radiating a long story

Now invite what is blotted
Disorder conceives of the joints
Lined last and forgotten
Etched against the garden gates

The evidence deteriorates
Leave me more
Than words to play with

Now give me what you promised.

Sit close don't bite
Heady realize
An expanse in her palms
A copy, a bird

Recreant firmament
Stitch me together
I'll cling to your hive

Now how long tell me
Is difference sustenance
And which words cage

Take a pen and ink and write it down

Here I'll lie
In a way
Where the matter begins

About the Author

Camille Guthrie was born in 1971 in Seattle, Washington. Her teenage years were spent in Pittsburgh, Pennsylvania. She received a B.A. in English Literature from Vassar College, and in 1996 she completed an M.F.A. at Brown University. She teaches at Friends Seminary in Manhattan and lives in Brooklyn. *The Master Thief* is her first book of poetry.